YOUR KNOWLEDGE HAS VALUE

Anusua Chowdhury

Cutting against the grain: Women in politics, picking up the gauntlet of nationalist struggle from-1857-1947

GRIN Verlag

Bibliografische Information der Deutschen Nationalbibliothek:

Die Deutsche Bibliothek verzeichnet diese Publikation in der Deutschen National-
bibliografie; detaillierte bibliografische Daten sind im Internet über http://dnb.d-
nb.de/ abrufbar.

Imprint:

Copyright © 2013 GRIN Verlag GmbH
Druck und Bindung: Books on Demand GmbH, Norderstedt Germany
ISBN: 978-3-656-53580-5

This book at GRIN:

http://www.grin.com/en/e-book/263802/cutting-against-the-grain-women-in-politics-
picking-up-the-gauntlet-of

GRIN - Your knowledge has value

Der GRIN Verlag publiziert seit 1998 wissenschaftliche Arbeiten von Studenten, Hochschullehrern und anderen Akademikern als eBook und gedrucktes Buch. Die Verlagswebsite www.grin.com ist die ideale Plattform zur Veröffentlichung von Hausarbeiten, Abschlussarbeiten, wissenschaftlichen Aufsätzen, Dissertationen und Fachbüchern.

Visit us on the internet:

http://www.grin.com/

http://www.facebook.com/grincom

http://www.twitter.com/grin_com

Cutting against the grain: Women in politics, picking up the gauntlet of nationalist struggle, from 1857-1947

Abstract:

The paper operates at the interstices of two main lines of inquiries: How far women were glorified in the context of Indian Nationalism? Why their heroism was blatantly camouflaged by male chauvinism? Multiple shades of heroism, heterogeneity of diverse cultures and religions were encapsulated in the early 20th cent. freedom movement of India. The paper unravels how the super-imposed patriarchy held women's actions at bay; and how in the last, they were drawn into the whirlpool of the movement. Nonetheless, the subtlety of their heroism created a deep mark in the history of Modern India. The paper explores the integration of disparate ideological and political groupings; and an eclectic blend of women's aestheticism and the chivalrous masculinity of men.

Keywords: Indian Nationalism, Heroism, Freedom movement.

Introduction:

Freedom from the heinous British rule was not an easy task; it was occasioned by concatenation of circumstances. The historical literature illuminates the achievements of male political scions like—Gandhi, playing second fiddle to the unheard voices of the nation. A veritable conundrum often finds place in the historical discourse, how far women were glorified in the context of Indian Nationalism? Why the nationalist literature showed reluctance to enmesh women into the broader network of national movement. Does that mean women remain enshrouded in cloak and contributed nothing to the political gamble? This indicates the norm of patriarchy that permeated the whole gamut of nationalist politics. Vidyamali Samarsinghe argues, 'at the most fundamental level, the public or productive sphere is male preserve, and the private sphere identified interchangeably as the re-productive sphere is designated venue of women'. [1] A plethora of cultural norms and myths successfully kept 'women' away from the domain of politics. Paradoxically, the metaphor of 'mother-goddess' was inscribed in nationalist politics; but in reality how far they were empowered? This is incumbent on me to find whether this seemingly disenfranchised group created space in the growing pantheon of nationalist politics.

---

[1] Vidyamali Samarsinghe, Subverting patriarchy? Leadership and participation of women in politics in South Asia, 2000, www.ices.lk/publications/esr/articles_jul00/ESR_2_-Vidya.3.pdf

Radha Kumar puts in, the 19th cent was the period of women; when the rights and wrongs of women were deplored and her potentialities and capabilities became the nature of heated discussions. With the turn of the century, 'women's question' was possibly numbed, as the overwhelming issues were directly political ones, concerning the politics of nationalism. Therefore, there was a perceptible decline in the reform movements as popular attitudes towards them hardened.

The development of Indian National Congress (1885) was concurrent with another intellectual and religious movement which was brought into logical culmination in the early half of the 20th cent. The movement, fashioned as 'religious revivalism' bore an indelible impression on the minds of rising extremists. They intended to define Hindu nation in terms of religion, myth and history. The main point of contrast between the two trends of the Congress was, 'reforms' inspired by the post-enlightenment influenced the agenda of Moderates. But the extremists developed a new aspect of anti-reformism, based on the concept of glorification of Hindu civilization.

The struggle for independence from the alien yoke was based on a tidal wave of nationalism, and the cultural icons had been proliferating throughout the country. Sucheta Mazumdar argues 'anti-colonialist national movement repeated and retrieved pre-colonial symbols and invented national cultures through which to challenge the cultural hegemony of the colonizer'.[2] They wanted the traditional imagery of women as docile and submissive being should remain unchangeable. Samarsinghe puts in, 'notions of Indian womanhood, entrenched in the private sphere, glorified as subservient, docile and sacrificial became an icon of Indian nationalist aspirations.'[3] The nationalists situated 'women's question' in an inner domain of political sovereignty, far removed from the arena of political contest with the colonial state. Partha Chatterjee has argued that the nationalist construction of the public and private spaces equated them with the material/spiritual dichotomy. The "world" or the public space, a typically male domain, was the site of contest and negotiation with the modernizing colonial state, while the "home" was the inner domain of sovereignty, which was beyond colonization, where women were perceived as the protector and nurturer of the spiritual essence of Indian national identity.[4] The image they projected here of womanhood, by and large, contributed in mobilizing patriarchal norms. However, women's strength and solidarity towards nation represented an important current of the political culture of pre-independent India. Women, in general, stood as the embodiment of purity and aestheticism. In fact, there were potential women who reportedly countered the patriarchal hegemony imposed by the westernised upper class men clustering around the English throne.

---

[2] Sucheta Mazumdar, Women, culture and politics, engendering the Hindu Nation, Comparative studies of South Asia, Africa and Middle East.

[3] Samarsinghe, 2000

[4] Partha Chatterjee, The Nation and its fragments, 1993: 116-34.

Testing the mettle:

The period from 1857 to 1947 saw the mastery of most of the nations, (particularly England), of the western hemisphere over the eastern half of the world. From 1857 on, the British Imperialism in India had a glimmering beginning, punctuated by drainage of wealth, official handicap of national economy, explosion of national animosity and sporadic outbreak of violence.

Talking about the effectiveness of women in politics, there was surely no dearth of astral feminine figures that leaped into the bandwagon of success. My purpose is to cast some fresh light upon the complex of intimately interrelated events spearheaded by women. To start with, the year 1857 had a mesmeric hold over the Indian imagination. The image of a valiant, feisty woman warrior on horseback, sabotaging the efforts of the British to conquer Jhansi is embedded in the historical narrative. Laxmibai's success crowned her efforts, the far she had gone, tracking the secure ways over the pathless seas; the very stars being the witnesses and testimonials of her triumph. The intrepidity and doughtiness that she showed in the battle-ground, doubtless, marks an important stage in the history of India, contradicting the image of a coy woman. The queen's courage and her firm resolution to retaining the kingdom of Jhansi from the British exacerbated tensions on both sides. To quote Indrani Sen, 'the colonial imagination was fascinated by the image of the fearless warrior woman who had fought with such audacious courage in battle'.[5] The name of Rani Laxmi bai is indissolubly associated with the Revolt of 1857, which is characterized as the most severe outburst of anger and discontent accumulated in the hearts of diverse sections of Indians ever since the inception of British rule. The centrality of her character stood as the emblem of nationalist aspiration and patriotic resistance. Late in the 19th cent another poignant figure, Swarna Kumari Devi, started her career as an editor in a family magazine "bharati". Jogesh Chandra Bagal argues, she was the first woman who participated publicly in the sessions of Indian National Congress between 1889 and 1890.[6] Running to the phase of Extremism and Swadeshi in Bengal, a famous Bengali face, Swarladebi Chaudhurani shunted aside long-drawn prejudices and captured the saddle of the revolutionary movement in Bengal. Her interpretation of nationalism was clearly built on a muscular, martial and poised male body. She invoked the courage and prowess in women and repeatedly urged them to remember they were but parts of Durga, the warrior goddess. Cutting against the grain, she was the first woman who initiated a gymnasium culture and became a member of the Anushilan samity in Mymensingh. Her many fallen leaves remained a chiaroscuro of a life well experienced- very rare for most women of her times.[7] To commemorate her act of bravery, S.N Banerjee felicitously commented: "The Indian ideal of womanhood is at once elevating and inspiring one, and fortunately it is not extinct yet".[8]

---

[5] Indrani Sen, Inscribing the Rani of Jhansi in Colonial 'mutiny' fiction, Economic and Political Weekly, pg-254

[6] Jogesh Chandra Bagal, Rashtriya Andolane Banga Mahila, (Bengali), Bethune College and School centenary volume , edited by Kalidas Nag,

[7] The scattered leaves of my life, An Indian Nationalist remembers, author: Swarladebi chaudhurani translated and edited by Sikita Banerjee, published by women unlimited, Stree, 2012.

[8] The Bengali, 28 November 1903.

The national movement took a momentous turn with the partition of Bengal in 1905. Mrs. Nonibala Debi joined the yugantar party which was dedicated to a violent movement in early 20th cent. Like her, women joined men in protesting this division by boycotting foreign goods and buying only indigenous goods, i.e. goods produced in the province of Bengal. Nonibala Devi hid defensive weapons and sheltered fugitives. Nirod C.Chaudhuri in The autobiography of an unknown Indian, "recalls how his mother was abstained from using foreign outfits, water-glass". Geraldine Forbes argues, in the anti-partition movement women had no definite role to play, except being the carrier of weapons, boycotting foreign goods, while the main part was master-minded by their male counterpart.[9]

Road to Militant Nationalism:

The militant nationalism, entrenched in Bomb politics and revolutionary movement dubbed as terrorism was the rising phenomenon in Bengal which subsequently permeated other parts of India. The cataclysm involved women of all levels, particularly the better-offs, albeit the incidence of participation of women in the first phase of the revolutionary movement was not remarkable. The pace of women's participation, however, accelerated from the late 1920s. Young girls began to join corps, take part in actions and created consternation in the broader canvass of nationalism. In Bengal, meanwhile, goddess-centred nationalist rhetoric gained momentum as the extremism expanded to terrorism and bomb-politics. They invoked the worship of mother-deity, kali symbolizing mother India. Radha Kumar puts in, Saraladevi, an active member of Mymensingh Suhrid samiti, began to be lauded for her puja to kali as pratapaditya's tutelary goddess. Other promising women revolutionaries who wonderfully conceived gun-powder plot are like, Madame Cama was actively involved in the revolutionary movement in India and abroad, with Shyamji Krishna Verma, S.R Rama and others. Among other activities she smuggled revolvers concealed in toys (sent as Christmas presents) to India. In 1907 she attended the International Socialist congress at Stuttgart, where she unfurled the Indian national flag and persuaded the congress to support Indian independence. Hemchandra kanungo, a member of Yugantar party in Calcutta, went abroad in Paris to train himself in military tactics and came in close encounter with this revolutionary party of which Madame Cama was a part.

Radha Kumar argues, as the rhetoric of Bengali nationalism grew increasingly mother-cantered more and more women participated in nationalist struggles. They were involved in nationalist activities, carrying weapons, sheltering revolutionaries and acting as couriers for extremists. Manmohun Kaur put in, Kaumudhini Mitra, an editor of Suprabhat, herself organised a cohort of active ladies who sheltered revolutionaries. Prabhavati Mirza, profoundly influenced by her brother's involvement in revolutionary movement spear-headed by Aurobindo Ghose. She fasted with many other at the hanging of Khudiram Bose and then Satyen Bose. Kamini Roy was active in illbert Bill agitation and Aghorekamini Roy campaigned against the ill-treatment of women worker in Assam, a cause which was first

---

[9] Geraldine Forbes, Women in Modern India, New Cambridge History of India.

espoused by the nationalist's in1880s. Speaking in a nutshell, women, being overwhelmed by the nationalist impulse, joined the spirit of the movement.

With the start of Gandhian politics, the nascent nationalism had acquired further momentum, climaxing with the quit India Movement in 1942. It was Gandhi who united the 'fragmented' voices of women across India with a common thread. Anup Taneja puts in, "Gandhi's basic philosophy was to negate aggressive, muscular stereotypes of human potential while incorporating the gentle, peaceful, communitarian aspects normally associated with women".[10] It was during his time that we see an upsurge in women politicization. At the clarion call of Gandhi thousands of women were drawn into the vortex of the freedom movement, sometimes defying the household chore. Women played an especially crucial role in the economic boycott campaigns and often participated in the non-cooperation movement with as much or even greater enthusiasm than their husbands or male relatives. In rallies organized by the Congress, women attended in large numbers often with little children in tow. As Geraldine Forbes puts in, Gandhi evoked India's sacred legends particularly the Ramayana, when he asked the Hindu women to join the movement, comparing women with brave 'sita' united with men against the immoral ruler, Ravana. Srimati Ambujammal, one of Gandhi's followers from Madras, outlined how Gandhi touched the hearts of both Hindu and Muslim women. First, he explained to women that they deserved a place in the freedom movement, secondly, he expressed faith in courage and tenacity and at the same time he re-assured families their women would not sacrifice family honour or prestige. Sucheta Kripalani credited Gandhi for his attitudes towards male. She argues that Gandhi's personality was such that it not only inspired women but also instilled a spirit of confidence in their guardians like -father, husband and brother.

In the Non-cooperation movement of 1921, Sarojini Naidu addressed women's crowd and decided to form their own political organization required to join the District Congress Committee. The committee was joined by several women of high repute, among them mention should be made of, Urmila Devi, widowed sister of C.R Das, Basanti devi, wife of C.R Das. By November 1000 Bombay women started demonstrations during the visit of Prince of Wales to India. At the All-India Ladies Conference in Ahmadabad 6000 women listened to Bi-Amma, the mother of Shaukat Ali and Md.Ali, the leaders of the Khilafat Movement. Sarla Devi, Muthulaxmi Reddy, Rajkumari Amrit Kaur, Susheela Nair, Sucheta Kripalani and Aruna Asaf Ali are some of the women who participated in the non-violent movement. Kasturba Gandhi, the illustrious wife of Mahatma Gandhi, and the women of the Nehru family, Kamla Nehru, wife of Jawaharlal Nehru, Mrs. Vijayalaxmi Pandit, his sister and Swarup Rani, his mother also joined the National Movement. Lado Rani Zutshi and her daughters Manmohini, Shyama and Janak led the movement in Lahore. Women who joined the national movement were not only from the higher strata of Indian society, but from all walks of life, all castes, religions and communities.

---

[10] Anup Taneja ,Gandhi, women and the National Movement,1920-47.,(published by Har Anand Publications ,2005) pg 60

Furthermore, by choosing the spinning wheel and salt as emblem of the freedom struggle and the civil disobedience movement, Madhu Kishwar, notes, "it is significant that all of Gandhi's symbols of struggles and protest were from the feminine reproductive realm, namely, spinning, picketing of liquor shops, and picking on salt as a symbol of countrywide Satyagraha (non violent civil disobedience)". [11]Actively encouraged by male political stalwarts such as Gandhi and Nehru, the Indian nationalist movement drew large numbers of women activists who did participate in all aspects of the struggle. At the same time Kumari Jayawardena argues "while Indian women were to participate in all stages of movement for national independence, they did so in a way that was acceptable to, and was directed by male leaders and which conformed to the prevalent ideology on the position of women".[12] A poignant affirmation of the prevailing patriarchal norms and women's accepted location in the private sphere was uttered by Sarojini Naidu (1870--1949), a most prominent woman activist of the time. Sucheta Mazumdar in her work quoted Naidu, "remember that in all great national crises it is the man who goes out, but it's the woman's hope and woman's prayer that serve his arm to become a successful soldier".[13] During the struggle for independence in India, women who came into the political arena did not deviate from norms of womanhood identified by a male dominant society.

There are some prominent instances of leadership, during the Chittagong armory raid some gallant women like Preetilata wardeha master-minded an attack against a European Club and later on, committed a suicide. Preetilata's Suicide testament, 24th September, 1932, says, "I wonder why there should be any distinction between males and females in a fight for the cause of the country's freedom? If our brothers can join a fight for the cause of the motherland why can't the sisters?

If sisters can stand side by side with the brothers in a movement, why are they not so entitled in a revolutionary movement?" [14] Kalpana Dutta, another member of Surya sen's revolutionary camp, courted an arrest. Released from the bar she joined the communist Party and later married P.C Joshi. The Statesman in a column, The History to remember, reported," Kalpana was a woman who had admirable energy, imagination and a sense of humour".[15]

History shows instances when important men took pride in their woman's participation, like Nehru boasted of his wife Kamala's arrest during civil disobedience days. He sent the following message to his daughter, Indira, as quoted in Promilla Kalhan, Kamala Nehru, an intimate biography, 1990,"Mummie is thoroughly happy and contended, it was a pleasant

[11] Madhu kishwar, "Women in Politics: Beyond Quotas," Economic and Political Weekly, Volume XXX1,

[12] Kumar Jayawardena, Feminism and Nationalism in the Third World, London, (Published by Zed Books, 1986) pg 108.

[13] Sucheta Mazumdar, Women ,culture and politics, engendering the Hindu Nation, Comparative Studies of South Asia, Africa and the Middle East Fall 1992 12(2): 1-24; cssaame.dukejournals.org/content/12/2/1.full.pdf

[14] Mandal, Women Revolutionaries , pg-4

[15] The Statesman, The History to remember.

new year gift for me"[16].....Nehru was happy as Kamala was not trailing her as a devoted wife; neither had she looked into her participation as an extension of her household chore. Looking to another hue of nationalism, The Indian National Army (INA), which was set up by Netaji Subhash Chandra Bose, was one of the most sincere and fearless movements undertaken by Indian men and women under the impressive leadership of this great patriot. Netaji Subhash Chandra Bose recruited about 1000 women for the Rank of Jhansi Regiment from different South East Asian countries. This regiment was led by Dr. Lakshmi Swaminathan, who was a medical doctor by profession. There were ranis as young as Janaki Davar who joined the INA at the age of seventeen. The women in the regiment were given the same training as that given to men. Even their uniform was similar to the men soldiers. The real impact of the INA may not have been in military terms, but it had a psychological impact on the women of India.

Undoubtedly, the ember of nationalism was roused in the mind of women and their valorising acts had stumped the nation. However, a review of women's role during the interlude of British rule has undertones of repressed feminism.

Vidyamali Samarasinghe argues," women's activities in the private sphere were so time-consuming that it hardly left women time to get involved in political activities of the public sphere".[17] Therefore, the 'equilibrium' between private and public sphere could not be maintained. However, women ventured to transcend the domestic boundary, sometimes crossing their in-laws, accentuating domestic tensions. For instance, the life of Nehru women was ridden with conflicts and ambiguities. The domestic life of Vijayalaxmi Pandit was endangered. Vijaylakshmi writes: "This was a time of great domestic strain, and constant adjustments and compromises were called for......." (Pandit. 1967-69)[18].

Concluding the essay, it is important to assess how far women were glorified in Indian Nationalism? Except few singular leaderships and some activities of glorious ladies from upper-middle stratum under the banner of Gandhi clinched in the historical discourse, there is no proof of an ordinary woman successfully surpassing Gandhi in politics. In fact Gandhi wanted women to follow his vestige, while he was their protégé. His wife Kasturba even never ventured to occupy the upper hand in politics; she followed the shadow of the political maestro and had left behind less visible trail. The picture of women portrayed in the canvass of Indian Nationalism is indeed bland and diluted. The Indian culture had always been very patria-linear. As it was gender normative so each gender was expected to conform to some prescribed social mores that gradually became more or less stereotypical. As for man, acts of bravery and chivalrous nature seen as an emblem of valorisation, likewise, for women 'sacrifice' was the main criterion of valorisation. We find an 'unbroken' link between

---

[16] Promila Kalhan, Kamala Nehru

[17] Vidyamali Samarasinghe, "Counting Women's Work: Intersection of Time and Space" in John Paul Jones III, Heidi Nast and Susan M Roberts (eds), Thresholds in Feminist Geography: Difference, Methodology and Representation, Lanham, Rowman and Littlefield, 1997, pp 129-144;

[18] Suruchi Thapar, The Nehru Women, Conflicts and Stresses During the Freedom Movement, www.manushi-india.org/pdfs_issues/.../the_nehru_women.pdf

women and lower-caste people. Eleanor Ross puts in "just as the woman is unable to escape the expectation of her gender, so too is the untouchable unable to escape his caste, it being acquired at birth and non-changeable".[19] She goes on narrating Spivak's work in her essay and how far the sentence "white men saved brown women from brown men", reflected in the British dealings with India. Doubtless, Spivak engages with the sati victims of the early colonial period and when nationalism was in an embryonic stage. In her work she has shown women through the prism of subaltern.   However this is true to the case of women during the later phase also, as they were unable to break the prejudiced wall constituted by the male society. Unfolding the original design, woman in being, as an entity was hardly glorified, but the feminine property of sacrifice, endurance were essential zed by the nationalist heroes and fitted it into the framework of non-violent movement. As Anup Taneja argues," these were the principal symbols that our political guru, Gandhi capitalized to mobilize large scale women to join the spirit of the movement only for the sake of country's freedom."[20] Woman was the paragon of the spiritual revolution and so, their aesthetic presence added a feather in the cap of nationalists. Precisely, woman was the secondary voice fighting under someone's aegis while their direct political action was held in abeyance.

---

[19] Eleanor Ross, 'Leading undergraduate work in English Studies,'volume2, 2009-10,ISN-2041-6776, http://www.nottingham.ac.uk/english/documents/innervate/09-10/0910rosssubaltern.pdf
[20] Taneja, Pg -72

Notes

1. Vidyamali Samarsinghe, Subverting patriarchy? Leadership and participation of women in politics in South Asia, 2000, www.ices.lk/publications/esr/articles_jul00/ESR_2_-Vidya.3.pdf

2. Radha Kumar, The History of Doing: An Illustrated account of Movements for Women's rights and Feminism in India, 1800-1990, Published by Kali for Women, 1993.

3. Sekhar Banerjee, From Plassey to Partition: A History of Modern India, published by Orient Longman, 2004.

4. Sucheta Mazumdar, Women, culture and politics, Comparative studies of South Asia, Africa and the Middle East.

5. Indrani Sen, Inscribing the Rani of Jhansi in colonial 'Mutiny' fiction, 1857, Essays from Economic and Political Weekly.

6. Jogesh Chandra Bagal, Rashtriya Andalone Banga Mahila (woman), Bethune College and school centenary volume, edited by Kalidas Nag.

7. S.N Banerjee, the Bengali, 28 November, 1903.

8. Geraldine Forbes, Women in Modern India, Cambridge History of Modern India.

9. Anup Taneja, Gandhi, Women and National movement, 1920-47, published by Har Anand Publications, 2005.

10. Madhu kishwar, "Women in Politics: Beyond Quotas," Economic and Political Weekly, Volume XXX1.

11. Kumar Jayawardena, Feminism and Nationalism in the Third World; Published by Zed Books, 1986.

12. For Preetilata Suicide testament, see Tirtha Mandal, Women revolutionaries in Bengal, 1905-39, published by Minerva Associates, one edition, April 1991.

13. Promilla kalhan, Kamala Nehru, An intimate autobiography, Vikas Publishing House, 1973, Delhi.

14. Suruchi Thapar, Nehru Women, Conflicts and Stresses during the Freedom Movement, Manushi, 1993.

15. Eleanor Ross, 'Leading undergraduate work in English Studies,'volume2, 2009-10, ISN-2041-6776.

16. Partha Chatterjee, Nation and its Fragments 1993, Princeton University Press.